ANNE OF GREEN GABLES

'Carrots! Carrots!' whispers Gilbert Blythe across the school desk, and he puts out his arm and pulls Anne's long red plaits. But Anne jumps up and cries, 'You horrible boy! I hate you!' And she hits him hard over the head with her book.

Life in the sleepy village of Avonlea is never boring after Anne Shirley comes to live with the Cuthberts. They wanted to adopt an orphan boy, to help with the farm work at Green Gables. But instead, they get Anne, who has red hair and freckles and who never stops talking. She's a loving child, but she's always in trouble! There's the visit from Mrs Lynde, then the cake for the vicar's wife, and the trouble with her hair . . .

And after the fight at school, will she ever speak to Gilbert Blythe again?

OXFORD BOOKWORMS LIBRARY
Human Interest

Anne of Green Gables

Stage 2 (700 headwords)

Series Editor: Jennifer Bassett
Founder Editor: Tricia Hedge
Activities Editors: Jennifer Bassett and Alison Baxter

L. M. MONTGOMERY

Anne of Green Gables

Retold by
Clare West

Illustrated by
Kate Simpson

OXFORD UNIVERSITY PRESS

OXFORD

UNIVERSITY PRESS

Great Clarendon Street, Oxford OX2 6DP

Oxford University Press is a department of the University of Oxford.
It furthers the University's objective of excellence in research, scholarship,
and education by publishing worldwide in

Oxford New York

Auckland Cape Town Dar es Salaam Hong Kong Karachi
Kuala Lumpur Madrid Melbourne Mexico City Nairobi
New Delhi Shanghai Taipei Toronto

With offices in

Argentina Austria Brazil Chile Czech Republic France Greece
Guatemala Hungary Italy Japan Poland Portugal Singapore
South Korea Switzerland Thailand Turkey Ukraine Vietnam

OXFORD and OXFORD ENGLISH are registered trade marks of
Oxford University Press in the UK and in certain other countries

ISBN 978 0 19 479052 9

A complete recording of this Bookworms edition of
Anne of Green Gables is available.

Typeset by Wyvern Typesetting Ltd, Bristol

Printed in China

Illustration on p49 by: David Eaton

Word count (main text): 5860 words

For more information on the Oxford Bookworms Library,
visit www.oup.com/elt/gradedreaders

CONTENTS

— 1 —

A surprise for the Cuthberts

Matthew Cuthbert lived with his sister Marilla on their farm on Prince Edward Island in Canada. Their farmhouse, Green Gables, was just outside the little village of Avonlea. Matthew was nearly sixty and had a long brown beard. His sister was five years younger. They were both tall and thin, with dark hair. Everybody in Avonlea knew that the Cuthberts were quiet people who worked very hard on their farm.

One afternoon Matthew drove the horse and cart to the station. 'Has the five-thirty train arrived yet?' he asked the station-master.

One afternoon Matthew drove the horse and cart to the station.

'Yes,' the man replied. 'And there's a passenger who's waiting for you. A little girl.'

'A little girl?' asked Matthew. 'But I've come for a boy! The children's home is sending us one of their orphan boys. We're going to adopt him, you see, and he's going to help me with the farm work.'

'Well, perhaps the children's home didn't have any boys, so they sent you a girl,' answered the station-master carelessly. 'Here she is.'

Matthew turned shyly to speak to the child. She was about eleven, with long red hair in two plaits. Her face was small, white and thin, with a lot of freckles, and she had large grey-green eyes. She was wearing an old brown hat and a dress which was too small for her.

'Are you Mr Cuthbert of Green Gables?' she asked excitedly in a high, sweet voice. 'I'm very happy to come and live with you, and belong to you. I've never belonged to anyone, you see. The people at the children's home were very kind, but it's not very exciting to live in a place like that, is it?'

Matthew felt sorry for the child. How could he tell her that it was all a mistake? But he couldn't just leave her at the station. He decided to take her home with him. Marilla could explain the mistake to her.

He was surprised that he enjoyed the journey home. He was a quiet, shy man, and he didn't like talking

'They sent you a girl,' said the station-master.

himself. But today, he only had to listen, because the little girl talked and talked and talked. She told him all about herself while they drove along.

'My parents died when I was a baby, you know, and for the last three years I've had to work for my food. I've lived with three different families and looked after their children. So I've always been poor, and I haven't got any nice dresses! But I just imagine that I'm wearing the most beautiful blue dress, and a big hat with flowers on, and blue shoes, and then I'm happy! Do you imagine things sometimes?'

'Well, I . . . I . . . not often,' said Matthew.

'I just imagine that I'm wearing the most beautiful blue dress.'

They were now driving past some very old apple trees next to the road. The trees were full of sweet-smelling, snowy-white flowers. The little girl looked at them.

'Aren't the trees beautiful?' she said happily. 'But am I talking too much? Please tell me. I *can* stop if necessary, you know.'

Matthew smiled at her. 'You go on talking,' he answered. 'I like listening to you.'

When they arrived at Green Gables, Marilla came to the door to meet them. But when she saw the little girl, she cried in surprise, 'Matthew, who's that? Where's the boy?'

'The children's home has made a mistake,' he said unhappily, 'and sent a girl, not a boy.'

The child was listening carefully. Suddenly she put her head in her hands and began to cry.

'You – you don't want me! ' she sobbed. ' Oh – oh! You don't want me because I'm not a boy!'

'Now, now, don't cry,' said Marilla kindly.

'Don't you understand? Oh! This is the worst thing that's happened to me in all my life!'

'Well, you can stay here, just for tonight,' said Marilla. 'Now, what's your name?'

The child stopped crying. 'Will you please call me Cordelia?' she asked.

'Call you Cordelia? Is that your name?'

'Well, no, it isn't, but it's a very beautiful name, isn't it? I like to imagine my name is Cordelia, because my real name is Anne Shirley – and that's not a very interesting name, is it?'

Marilla shook her head. 'The child has too much imagination,' she thought.

'Well, you can stay here, just for tonight,' said Marilla.

Later, when Anne was in bed, Marilla said to her brother, 'She must go back to the children's home tomorrow.'

'Marilla, don't you think . . .' began Matthew. 'She's a nice little thing, you know.'

'Matthew Cuthbert, are you telling me that you want to keep her?' asked Marilla crossly.

Matthew looked uncomfortable. 'Well, she's clever, and interesting, and—'

'But we don't need a girl!'

'But perhaps she needs us,' Matthew replied, surprisingly quickly for him. 'She's had a very unhappy life up to now, Marilla. She can help you in the house. I can get a boy from the village to help me on the farm. What do you think?'

Marilla thought for a long time. 'All right,' she said in the end, 'I agree. The poor child can stay. I'll look after her.'

Matthew smiled happily. 'Be as good and kind to her as you can, Marilla. I think she needs a lot of love.'

—— 2 ——
At Green Gables

And so the next morning Marilla said, 'Well, Anne, Matthew and I have decided to keep you, only if you're a good girl, of course. Why, child, what's the matter?'

'I'm crying,' sobbed Anne, 'because I'm very happy! It's beautiful here! People say I'm very bad, but I'll try very hard to be good. Oh, thank you! Thank you!'

'Now stop crying, child,' said Marilla a little crossly, 'and listen. We're going to adopt you, and send you to school after the summer holidays.'

Anne stopped crying. 'Can I call you Aunt Marilla? I've never had any family at all, so I'd really like to have an aunt. We could imagine that you're my mother's sister.'

'*I* couldn't,' answered Marilla firmly.

'Don't you imagine things?' asked Anne, surprised.

'No, I don't,' Marilla replied. 'I do my housework, and look after Matthew, and go to church on Sunday. There's no time for imagining things in this house. Just remember that, Anne.'

Anne was silent for a few minutes. Then she said, 'Marilla, do you think I'll find a best friend in Avonlea? Someone who really understands me and knows all my secrets. I've always wanted a friend like that.'

'Our friends, the Barrys, have a daughter called Diana, who's eleven, like you. But if you want to play with her, you'll have to be very good. Mrs Barry is very careful about Diana's friends.'

'Diana! What a beautiful name!' said Anne excitedly. 'Her hair isn't red, is it? I hope it isn't.' She looked sadly at her red plaits. 'I hate *my* hair.'

'Diana has dark hair. She's a good, clever girl. Try to be like her, Anne.'

When the two girls met, they knew at once that they would be good friends. They often played together, in the fields, or by the river, or in the garden. In the morning Anne helped Marilla with the housework. Then in the afternoon she played with Diana, or talked happily to Matthew while he worked on the farm. She soon knew and loved every flower, tree, and animal at Green Gables.

In the morning Anne helped Marilla with the housework.

The Cuthberts had another friend, Mrs Rachel Lynde. She liked to know everything that was happening in and around Avonlea. She was very interested in the Cuthberts' little orphan girl, so one day she visited Marilla.

'I was very surprised to hear about the child,' she told Marilla. 'So you and Matthew have adopted her!'

'I'm surprised myself,' answered Marilla with a smile. 'But she's a clever little thing, you know. And she's always dancing, or singing, or laughing.'

Mrs Lynde shook her head sadly. 'What a mistake, Marilla! You've never had any children yourself, so how can you look after her?'

Just then Anne ran in from the garden. She stopped suddenly when she saw a stranger in the kitchen. Mrs Lynde looked at the thin little girl in the short dress, with her freckled face and red hair.

'Isn't she thin, Marilla?' she said. 'Just look at those freckles! And hair as red as carrots!'

Anne's face went red. She ran up to Mrs Lynde.

'I hate you!' she shouted angrily. 'I hate you! You're a horrible, fat old woman!' And she ran upstairs.

'Oh dear, oh dear!' said Mrs Lynde. 'What a terrible child! You'll not have an easy time with her, Marilla.'

'You were rude to her, Rachel,' Marilla replied, before she could stop herself.

'Well!' said Mrs Lynde. She got up and walked to

the door. 'I think this orphan is more important to you than I am. When I think how long we've been friends . . . You'll have trouble with her, I can tell you. Well, I'm sorry for you, that's all. Goodbye.'

Marilla went upstairs to Anne's room. The child was lying on her narrow bed, sobbing loudly.

'You mustn't get angry like that, Anne. Mrs Lynde is my friend, and you were very rude to her.'

Anne was lying on her narrow bed, sobbing loudly.

'*She* was rude to *me*!' said Anne. 'She said I was thin and freckled and red-haired. It was very unkind!'

'I understand how you feel,' said Marilla. 'But you must go to her and tell her you're sorry.'

'I can never do that,' said Anne firmly.

'Then you must stay in your room and think about it. You can come out when you agree to say that you're sorry.'

Anne stayed in her room all the next day. Downstairs the house was very quiet without her. That evening, while Marilla was busy in the garden, Matthew went up to Anne's room. The child was sitting sadly by the window.

'Anne,' he said shyly, 'why don't you say you're sorry? Then you can come down, and we can all be happy.'

'I *am* sorry now,' said Anne. 'I was very angry yesterday! But do you really want me to . . .'

'Yes, do, please. It's lonely downstairs without you. But don't tell Marilla I've talked to you.'

Marilla was pleased to hear that Anne was sorry. Later that evening, when she and Anne were in Mrs Lynde's warm kitchen, Anne suddenly fell on her knees.

'Oh Mrs Lynde,' cried the little girl, 'I'm very sorry. I can't tell you how sorry I am, so you must just imagine it. I *am* a bad girl! But please say you will forgive me. I'll be sad all my life if you don't!'

Anne suddenly fell on her knees.

'She's enjoying herself!' thought Marilla, watching Anne's face. 'She doesn't look sorry at all, but happy and excited!'

But Mrs Lynde said kindly, 'Of course I forgive you.' And later she said to Marilla, 'Perhaps you're right to keep her. She's a strange little thing, but I think I like her.'

—— 3 ——
At Avonlea school

When school started in September, Anne and Diana walked there and back together every day.

'What a beautiful day,' Anne said happily one morning, as the two little girls walked across the fields. 'I'm very lucky to have you as my best friend, Diana. You *are* my best friend, aren't you?'

'Of course, Anne,' replied Diana, taking Anne's hand. 'And just think, today you'll meet Gilbert Blythe. He's three years older than us, and *very* good-looking. He's just come back from holiday, and starts school today.'

'Oh, boys!' said Anne. 'I'm not interested in *them*.' But she did look at Gilbert when they arrived at school. He was a tall boy, with curly brown hair and a friendly smile.

'He *is* good-looking,' Anne whispered to Diana, 'but why does he smile at me? He doesn't know me!'

Avonlea school was quiet that day. The teacher, Mr Phillips, was helping some of the older children at the back of the schoolroom. Anne was looking out of the window at the reds and yellows of the trees, and the silvery blue of the river. She was far away in the world of her imagination. But Gilbert wanted her to look at him. He whispered to her, but she did not move. He was

14

surprised. Girls were usually very ready to look at him.

Suddenly he put his arm out, pulled her red plaits, and said in a loud whisper, 'Carrots! Carrots!'

Anne jumped up and looked angrily at Gilbert.

'You horrible boy!' she cried. 'I hate you!' And then she brought her heavy book down on Gilbert's head.

Gilbert put his arm out, and pulled Anne's plaits.

Mr Phillips heard the noise, and came slowly to the front of the schoolroom.

'Anne Shirley, why did you do that?' he asked. She stayed silent. Gilbert said, 'I'm sorry, Mr Phillips. I was rude to her. That's why she hit me.' But the teacher did not listen to Gilbert.

'I cannot have bad children in my school,' said Mr Phillips firmly. 'Anne, go and stand in front of the class.' And there Anne stood for the rest of the day, a lonely little girl with a small white angry face.

'I hate Mr Phillips!' she thought. 'And I'll never look at or speak to Gilbert Blythe again!'

The next day some of the school children were playing in a farmer's field in their lunch hour, so they were a little late for afternoon school. Anne ran into the classroom at the same time as the boys, just after the teacher.

'You're late, Anne,' said Mr Phillips. 'You won't sit with Diana today. I see that you enjoy being with the boys very much, so go and sit next to Gilbert this afternoon.'

Anne's face went white. 'He can't mean it!' she thought.

'Did you hear me, Anne?' asked Mr Phillips.

'Yes sir,' said Anne and moved slowly to Gilbert's desk. There she sat down and put her head on the desk, with her arms over it.

'This is the end,' she was thinking. 'I wasn't the only person who was late. And he's sent me to sit with a *boy*! And that boy is Gilbert Blythe!'

The rest of the day went very slowly for Anne. When it was time to leave, she went to her desk, next to Diana's, and took all her books, pens and pencils with her.

'What are you doing, Anne?' asked Diana.

Anne took all her books, pens and pencils.

17

'I'm not coming back to school,' replied Anne firmly.

'Oh! But Anne . . . we're reading a new book next week . . . and we're playing a new game on Monday, and . . . It'll be very exciting! And you'll miss it, Anne!'

But Anne was not interested. 'I'm sorry, Diana,' was her only answer.

That evening Marilla ran round to Rachel Lynde's house. 'Rachel, please help me! Anne says she won't go back to school. What am I going to say to her?'

Mrs Lynde already knew about Anne's troubles at school, and she was always very pleased when people asked her to help. She smiled and sat back comfortably.

'I've had ten children myself, so I know all about them,' she said. 'Anne can stay at home for a while. She'll want to go back to school again soon, I'm sure.'

So Anne stayed at home, and only saw Diana in the evenings. She was a child who felt very strongly. She hated Gilbert Blythe, but she really loved Diana.

One evening Marilla found Anne crying in the kitchen. 'What's the matter, child?' she asked in surprise.

'I love Diana very much,' sobbed Anne. 'I can't live without her, Marilla! But what will happen when she marries? I hate her husband already! I can imagine her in the church in her long white dress . . . and then she'll go away! And I'll never see her again!'

Marilla turned away to hide her smiling face. What a

'Diana'll go away, and I'll never see her again!' sobbed Anne.

strange, funny child Anne was! Marilla tried not to laugh, but she couldn't stop herself.

'You and your imagination, Anne Shirley!' she cried, and she laughed and laughed.

Mrs Lynde was right, of course. After a few days Anne decided to go back to school. All the children were pleased to see her again, but she did not speak to Gilbert Blythe.

— 4 —
More trouble for Anne

'I think I'll ask the new vicar, Mr Allan, and his wife to tea on Wednesday,' said Marilla one day.

'Oh yes, please do!' cried Anne excitedly. 'Mrs Allan is young and beautiful, and has a very sweet smile! Can I make a cake for tea? Say yes, Marilla!'

Marilla agreed, and for the next few days Anne planned what she would put in her cake.

'I do hope it's going to be a good one,' she told Diana. 'Sometimes I forget to put in the right things.'

'You made a very good one last week,' said her friend. 'I'm sure it'll be all right.'

On Wednesday the tea party started very well.

'These are very good cakes, Miss Cuthbert,' Mrs Allan said to Marilla. 'You *have* been busy.'

'*Anne* made this one, specially for you, Mrs Allan,' replied Marilla.

'Oh well, I must try some,' laughed the vicar's wife. But after the first mouthful there was a very strange look on her face.

'Is anything wrong?' asked Marilla. She ate a piece of Anne's cake herself. 'Oh! Anne! What *have* you put in this cake?' she cried.

'Isn't it . . . isn't it all right?' asked Anne, her face red.

'Oh! Anne! What have you put in this cake?' Marilla cried.

'All right? It's horrible! Don't try to eat any more, Mrs Allan. Anne, you've put my medicine in this cake!'

'Oh! I didn't know! It was white, and in a bottle! I thought it was milk!' sobbed Anne. She ran upstairs and fell on her bed, crying loudly.

But later that evening, when Mr and Mrs Allan went home, Marilla came to talk to her.

'Oh Marilla!' cried Anne. 'Everybody in Avonlea will laugh at me for putting medicine in a cake!'

Marilla smiled and touched Anne's hot face. 'No, they won't, Anne. Mrs Allan wasn't angry, you know. She said it was very kind of you to make her a cake, and she's asked you to tea at her house!'

'Oh, so she's forgiven me! She *is* nice, isn't she?' said Anne thankfully. 'Why do I get into trouble like this? Perhaps I won't make any mistakes tomorrow.'

Marilla shook her head, still smiling. 'You'll think of something, Anne. You're very good at making mistakes!'

***

Spring came, with its bright green leaves and early flowers. One April evening Marilla came home late after visiting friends. She found the kitchen empty, and no supper on the table.

'Where's Anne?' she thought crossly. 'I told her to get the supper ready.' She hurried upstairs to Anne's room, and found the girl sobbing on her bed.

'Don't look at me, Marilla!' Anne cried. 'I know I'm bad, I know I am!'

'What *is* the matter?' asked Marilla. 'Are you ill?'

'Oh Marilla, I just want to die! *Look at my hair!*'

And Marilla saw that Anne's long thick red hair was now a horrible dark green.

'Oh Anne!' she said, 'What *have* you done now?'

'I . . . I bought a bottle of something special from a man who came to the door. He said it would change my hair from red to black! Oh, I know it was stupid of me! But what shall I do?'

*'I bought a bottle of something special from a man
who came to the door.'*

23

They washed Anne's hair again and again, but it was still green. Anne stayed at home for a week, saw nobody, and washed her hair every day. But at the end of the week, Marilla said, 'I'm sorry, Anne, we'll have to cut it all off. You can't go to school with green hair.'

'We'll have to cut it all off.'

Anne had to agree. 'Perhaps this will teach me not to think about being beautiful,' she said sadly.

Everybody was surprised to see Anne with very short hair, but no one learned the secret. And some weeks later, there were some new, darker red curls, which pleased Anne very much.

***

24

That summer Anne and her friends often played in an old boat on the river.

'Today, let's imagine that I'm a prisoner and I'm escaping from prison by boat,' said Anne. 'I'll hide in the boat and the river will carry it down to the bridge. You're my family, and you must meet me at the bridge.'

The other girls agreed, so Anne got into the boat and hid under some coats. Her friends pushed the boat off down the river and ran across the fields to get round to the bridge. For a few minutes the prisoner enjoyed the game, but then she suddenly felt wet and sat up. Water was coming in very fast through a hole in the bottom of the boat! Luckily, there were some trees by the river and Anne saw a low branch over the water. She jumped up and caught the branch. The boat went on without her and a few seconds later went down under the water.

Her friends on the bridge saw the boat, but they did not see Anne under the tree. 'Oh! Oh! Anne's dead! The boat's gone down and she's in the river!' they screamed, and ran back to the village for help.

Poor Anne could not move. She held on and held on, but her arms were getting tired and she knew that she would fall in a minute. Suddenly, there was Gilbert Blythe in his boat!

'Anne Shirley!' he cried. 'What *are* you doing there?' He did not wait for an answer, but quickly helped Anne

Suddenly, there was Gilbert Blythe in his boat!

into his boat. She didn't say a word. When they arrived at the bridge, she got out and turned away.

'Thank you for helping me,' she said coldly.

But Gilbert jumped out, and put a hand on her arm.

'Anne,' he said quickly, 'I'm sorry I called you "carrots". It was a long time ago. I think your hair is really nice now. Can we forget it, and be friends?'

For a second Anne wanted to say yes. But then she remembered standing alone in front of the school children all afternoon, because of Gilbert. She would never forgive him for that! 'No,' she replied coldly, 'I shall never be your friend, Gilbert Blythe!'

'All right!' Gilbert jumped angrily back into his boat. 'I'll never ask you again, Anne Shirley!'

Anne walked home with her head held high, but she felt strangely sad, and wanted to cry.

'Why are you always in trouble, Anne?' asked Marilla, when she heard about Anne's adventure.

'Well, I think I'm learning, Marilla,' answered Anne. 'I learn from my mistakes, and after today, I won't use my imagination so much. I don't think Avonlea is the right place for imagination.'

'No, it isn't,' agreed Marilla a little crossly.

When she went out, Matthew, who was sitting quietly in his corner, whispered to Anne, 'Keep a little imagination, Anne, not too much, of course, just a little.'

—— 5 ——
Queen's College

One day Marilla said, 'Anne, your new teacher, Miss Stacy, spoke to me yesterday. She says you must study for the examinations for Queen's College in two years' time. Then if you do well, you can study at Queen's in Charlottetown for a year, and after that you'll be a teacher!'

'Oh Marilla! I'd *love* to be a teacher! But won't it be very expensive?'

'That doesn't matter, Anne. When Matthew and I adopted you three years ago, we decided to look after you as well as we could. Of course we'll pay for you to study.'

So in the afternoons Anne and some of her friends stayed late at school, and Miss Stacy helped them with the special examination work. Diana didn't want to go to Queen's, so she went home early, but Gilbert stayed. He and Anne still never spoke and everybody knew that they were enemies, because they both wanted to be first in the examination. Secretly, Anne was sorry that she and Gilbert weren't friends, but it was too late now.

For two years Anne studied hard at school. She enjoyed learning, and Miss Stacy was pleased with her. But she didn't study all the time. In the evenings and at weekends she visited her friends, or walked through the fields with Diana, or sat talking to Matthew.

'Your Anne is a big girl now. She's taller than you,' Rachel Lynde told Marilla one day.

'You're right, Rachel!' said Marilla in surprise.

'And she's a very good girl now, isn't she? She doesn't get into trouble these days. I'm sure she helps you a lot with the housework, Marilla.'

'Yes, I don't know what I'd do without her,' said Marilla, smiling.

'And look at her! Those beautiful grey eyes, and that red-brown hair! You know, Marilla, I thought you and Matthew made a mistake when you adopted her. But

'Your Anne is a big girl now,' Rachel Lynde told Marilla.

now I see I was wrong. You've looked after her very well.'

'Well, thank you, Rachel,' replied Marilla, pleased.

That evening, when Matthew came into the kitchen, he saw that his sister was crying.

'What's the matter?' he asked, surprised. 'You haven't cried since . . . well, I can't remember when.'

'It's just . . . well, I was thinking about Anne,' said Marilla. 'I'll . . . I'll miss her when she goes away.'

'When she goes to Queen's, you mean? Yes, but she can come home at weekends, on the train.'

'I'll still miss her,' said Marilla sadly.

In June the Avonlea boys and girls had to go to Charlottetown to take their examinations.

'Oh, I do hope that I've done well,' Anne told Diana when she arrived back at Green Gables. 'The examinations were very difficult. And I've got to wait for three weeks before I know! *Three weeks*! I'll die!'

Anne wanted to do better than Gilbert. But she also wanted to do well for Matthew and Marilla. That was very important to her.

Diana was the first to hear the news. She ran into the kitchen at Green Gables and shouted, 'Look, Anne! It's in Father's newspaper! You're first . . . with Gilbert . . . out of all the students on the island! Oh, how wonderful!' Anne took the paper with shaking hands, and saw her name, at the top of the list of two hundred. She could not speak.

'Well, now, I knew it,' said Matthew with a warm smile.

'You've done well, I must say, Anne,' said Marilla, who was secretly very pleased.

'Look, Anne! It's in Father's newspaper!' shouted Diana.

For the next three weeks Anne and Marilla were very busy. Anne needed new dresses to take to Charlottetown.

The evening before she left, she put on one of her new dresses to show Matthew. Marilla watched the happy young face. She remembered the strange, thin little child, with her sad eyes, who arrived at Green Gables five years ago, and she started crying quietly.

Anne put on one of her new dresses to show Matthew.

'Marilla, why are you crying?' asked Anne.

'I was just thinking of you when you were a little girl,' said Marilla. 'And . . . you're going away now . . . and I'll be lonely without you.'

Anne took Marilla's face in her hands. 'Marilla, nothing will change. Perhaps I'm bigger and older now, but I'll always be your little Anne. And I'll love you and Matthew and Green Gables more every day of my life.'

Marilla could not say what she felt, like Anne, but she could show it. She put her arms round her girl and held her close to her heart.

And so for the next year Anne lived in Charlottetown, and went to college every day. She sometimes came home at weekends, but she had to study hard. Some of her Avonlea friends were at Queen's too, and also her enemy, Gilbert Blythe. Anne saw that he often walked and talked with other girls. She felt sure that she and Gilbert could have some interesting conversations. But she didn't want to be the first to speak to him, and he never looked at her.

There were examinations at the end of the college year, in May. Anne studied very hard for them.

'I'd love to get the first place,' she thought. 'Or perhaps I could get the Avery prize.' This was a prize for the student who was best at English writing, and Anne knew she was good at that. The Avery prize paid for a free place for four years at Redmond College, one of the best colleges in Canada.

When news of the examinations came, Anne waited for her friends to tell her. She heard shouting. 'It's Gilbert! He's the first!' She felt ill. But just then she heard another shout. 'Anne Shirley's got the Avery!' And then all the girls were round her, laughing and shouting.

'Matthew and Marilla will be pleased!' thought Anne. 'Now I can go on studying, and they won't have to pay!'

'Anne Shirley's got the Avery!'

—— 6 ——
Matthew and Marilla

But when she arrived back at Green Gables, Anne knew at once that something was wrong. Matthew looked much older than before.

'What's the matter with him?' Anne asked Marilla.

'He's had some heart trouble this year,' replied Marilla. 'He really isn't well. I'm worried about him.'

'And *you're* not looking well, Marilla,' said Anne. 'Now you must rest, while *I* do the housework.'

Marilla smiled tiredly at Anne. 'It's not the work, it's my head. It often hurts, behind my eyes. I must see the doctor about it soon. But another thing, Anne, have you heard anything about the Church Bank?'

'I heard it was having a difficult time.'

'All our money is in that bank. I know Matthew's worried about it.'

The next morning a letter came for Matthew. Marilla saw his grey face and cried, 'What's the matter, Matthew?'

Anne, who was bringing an armful of flowers into the kitchen, saw his face too. Suddenly, Matthew fell to the ground. Anne dropped her flowers and ran to help Marilla. Together they tried everything, but it was too late. Matthew was dead.

'It was his heart,' said the doctor, who arrived a little

Anne dropped her flowers and ran to help Marilla.

later. 'Did he have any bad news suddenly?'

'The letter!' cried Anne. 'Shall I see what's in it? Oh Marilla, look! The Church Bank has had to close down! Your money, and Matthew's, has all gone!'

Everybody in Avonlea was sorry to hear that Matthew was dead. For the first time in his life, Matthew Cuthbert was an important person.

At first Anne couldn't cry. But then she remembered Matthew's smiling face when she told him about the Avery prize. Suddenly she started crying and couldn't stop. Marilla held her in her arms and they sobbed together.

'Crying can't bring him back,' whispered Marilla. 'We'll have to learn to live without him, Anne.'

***

In the next few weeks Anne and Marilla worked hard together on the farm and in the house. Everybody in Avonlea was very kind to them, but it was a sad time.

One day Marilla said, 'I'll miss you when you go to Redmond College, Anne. What are the other Avonlea students going to do?'

'Some of them are going to teach, and some are going to stay at Queen's.'

'Gilbert's going to teach at Avonlea school, isn't he?' Anne didn't reply, so Marilla went on. 'He's very tall and good-looking now, don't you think? Like his father,

John, when he was younger. You know, John and I were very good friends, years ago.'

Anne looked up, interested. 'What happened? Why didn't you . . .?'

'Well, we had a fight about something. He asked me to be friends again, but I couldn't forgive him. Later I was sorry, but he didn't speak to me again. Perhaps we . . . Oh well, it was a long time ago.'

The next day Marilla went to see the doctor. When she came back, she looked very tired and ill.

'What did the doctor say?' asked Anne worriedly.

'He says I mustn't read or write, and I must wear glasses. Then my head won't hurt. But if I'm not very careful, I'll be blind in six months!'

'I mustn't read or write, and I must wear glasses.' said Marilla.

For a minute Anne was silent. Then she said firmly, 'Then you must be careful, Marilla.'

'Think how terrible it is to be blind! But how lucky you've got a free place at Redmond College! I can't give you any money, you see. All our money's gone, and I can't work now. I think I'll have to sell the farm, and go and live with Rachel Lynde!' and poor Marilla sobbed wildly.

That night Anne sat alone in her bedroom. She thought and thought for some time, and then she smiled. When she went to bed, she knew what she was going to do.

The next day she explained it all to Marilla.

'You can't sell Green Gables, it's our home! Just listen, I've planned everything. I'm not going to Redmond College, it's too far away. I'm going to teach, in one of the village schools near here. Then I can live there during the week and come home at weekends to look after you. Diana's father will use our fields and pay us for them, and so we'll have some money. You see?'

'Oh Anne! I'll be all right if *you're* here. But you *must* go to Redmond, if you want to study . . .'

'Redmond College doesn't matter,' laughed Anne. 'I'm going to study at home in the evenings. And I'm going to be a really good teacher! That's better than anything!'

Marilla shook her head and tried not to cry. 'You're a good girl, Anne. Now we can keep Green Gables!'

A few days later Rachel Lynde came to the farm.

'Do you know,' she said, 'that Gilbert isn't going to be the Avonlea teacher now?'

'Isn't he?' cried Anne. 'Why not?'

'When he heard that you wanted to be near Marilla, he decided to teach at a school in another village. So *you* can be the Avonlea teacher now.'

'Oh!' said Anne, surprised. 'That's . . . that's very kind of him.'

And that day, when she saw Gilbert by the river, she stopped him and held out her hand.

'Gilbert,' she said shyly, 'I . . . I want to thank you. It's very good of you. If I'm the Avonlea teacher, I can help Marilla much more at home.'

'I'm happy to help you, Anne,' said Gilbert. He smiled and held her hand firmly. 'Are we going to be friends now? Have you forgiven me for calling you "carrots"?'

Anne laughed. 'I forgave you a long time ago.'

'I'm sure we're going to be very good friends, Anne. Can I walk home with you?'

And when Anne came into the Green Gables kitchen, Marilla said, 'You look very happy, Anne. Was that Gilbert who was with you just now?'

'Yes,' replied Anne, her face red. 'Gilbert and I've

Gilbert smiled and held Anne's hand firmly.

decided to be friends. Oh Marilla, I think life is going to be good for all of us! We'll have to work hard, but we'll be happy. And we'll keep our dear old Green Gables! What could be better than that!'

GLOSSARY

adopt   to take the child of another person into your family to become your own child

beard   the hair on a man's face

blind   not able to see

branch   one of the 'arms' of a tree

college   a place where people go to study, after leaving school

examination   a test of what someone knows or can do

farm   fields and buildings where people grow food and keep animals

firmly   showing that you have decided something

forgive (past tense **forgave**)   to show or say that you are not angry with somebody any more

freckles   small brown marks on a person's skin (often on the face)

hate   opposite of love

heart   the part of your body that pushes the blood round

horrible   very bad

imagine   to make a picture of something in your head

knee   the part in the middle of your leg where it bends

medicine   a special drink that helps someone who is ill to get better

miss   to feel sad when someone has gone away

orphan   a child whose parents are dead; orphans often live in a children's home

plait   long pieces of hair put over and under each other to make one thick piece

prize   a kind of 'present' which somebody gets if they win or come first in something (e.g. an examination)

rude not polite

sad unhappy

shy not sure of yourself; finding it difficult to talk to people

sob (past tense **sobbed**) to cry loudly and very unhappily

study (past tense **studied**) to read, think, and learn

vicar a priest in the Protestant Church

whisper to speak very softly and quietly

worried feeling that something is wrong

ACTIVITIES

Before Reading

1 Read the story introduction on the first page of the book, and the back cover. How much do you know now about the people in the book?
Tick one of the boxes for each sentence.   YES   NO

 1 Marilla and Matthew are married.   ☐ ☐
 2 The Cuthberts wanted to adopt a boy.   ☐ ☐
 3 Anne likes eating carrots.   ☐ ☐
 4 Avonlea is a large town in the USA.   ☐ ☐
 5 Mrs Lynde comes to visit the Cuthberts.   ☐ ☐
 6 Gilbert Blythe is Anne's best friend.   ☐ ☐
 7 The Cuthberts' life changes after Anne comes
    to live with them.   ☐ ☐

2 This story takes place in Canada, about a hundred years ago. How do you think life was different then? Tick one box for each question.

                                                    YES   NO

 1 Could people travel from town to town by train? ☐ ☐
 2 Did country people drive cars?   ☐ ☐
 3 Did farmers and their families work hard?   ☐ ☐
 4 Did young children sometimes have to work?   ☐ ☐
 5 Did poor children go to school or college?   ☐ ☐

ACTIVITIES

While Reading

Read Chapter 1. Who said or thought this?

1 'Perhaps the children's home didn't have any boys.'
2 'You – you don't want me!'
3 'The child has too much imagination.'
4 'She's a nice little thing, you know.'
5 'But we don't need a girl!'

Read Chapter 2, and complete the sentences about the people who live in or near Avonlea.

1 _____ Cuthbert looks after her brother, _____.
2 The Cuthberts' friends are called the _____.
3 _____ Barry is eleven years old, just like _____.
4 Anne thought that _____ was a horrible, fat old woman.

Read Chapter 3, then answer these questions.

Who

1 . . . was Anne's best friend?
2 . . . was Anne's first teacher at school?
3 . . . called Anne 'carrots'?
4 . . . wanted to stay away from school?
5 . . . was happy to tell Marilla what to do?

Before you read Chapter 4, think about the title, which is *More trouble for Anne*. Can you guess what kind of trouble? Tick one box each time.

	YES	NO
1 forgetting to do her homework	☐	☐
2 making a cake that tastes bad	☐	☐
3 colouring her hair	☐	☐
4 being rude to Mrs Lynde	☐	☐
5 falling into a river	☐	☐
6 needing help from Gilbert	☐	☐

Read Chapter 5. Are these sentences true (T) or false (F)?

1 Diana studied for the Queen's College examinations too.

2 Marilla showed how much she loved Anne.

3 Anne came home every weekend from college.

4 Anne and Gilbert became friends.

5 Anne hoped to get the Avery prize.

Read Chapter 6. Choose the best question-word for these questions, and then answer them.

Where / What / Why

1 . . . was the matter with Matthew?

2 . . . did the letter from the Church Bank say?

3 . . . was Gilbert going to teach?

4 . . . didn't Marilla marry John Blythe years ago?

5 . . . did Anne decide to stay in Avonlea?

After Reading

1 **When Anne first arrived in Charlottetown, perhaps she wrote a letter to Marilla. Use these words from the story to complete the letter. (Use each word once.)**

cake, college, farm, forgive, girls, horrible, imagination, lonely, miss, prize, speak, studying, time, weekend, writing

Dear Marilla,

It's strange living here in a _____ with a lot of other _____, and not at dear old Green Gables! I really _____ you and Matthew! But you mustn't feel _____ without me, because I'll come home next _____ on the train.

The work is very interesting, and I'm _____ very hard. But there's also _____ to see my friends. Some other Avonlea girls are here, and of course, that _____ Gilbert Blythe too! I'll never _____ him for what happened at school. I don't _____ to him, and he never looks at me.

I'd really like to get the Avery _____ at the end of the year. That's for English _____, and I know I'm good at that, because I've got a lot of _____!

Look after Matthew and yourself, and make a big chocolate _____ for next weekend! I can't wait to come home, and see you both, and everything on the _____!

Love from Anne

2 Here is a new illustration for the story. Find the best place
   in the story to put the picture, and answer these questions.

The picture goes on page _____.

1 Who is the person in this picture?
2 What is happening at the moment?
3 What is going to happen next?

Now write a caption for the illustration.

Caption: _____

49

3 There are 25 words from the story hidden in this word search. How many can you find in ten minutes? Words can only run from top to bottom and from left to right.

Y	X	W	Y	H	O	O	G	M	P	B
G	S	F	R	E	C	K	L	E	S	L
K	T	J	Z	A	A	N	A	B	A	I
H	A	T	E	R	R	E	S	E	D	N
M	T	U	W	T	T	E	S	A	X	D
C	I	R	U	D	E	S	E	R	I	Q
C	O	L	L	E	G	E	S	D	P	S
B	N	C	U	R	L	Y	W	K	L	O
Q	M	F	O	R	G	I	V	E	A	B
C	A	K	E	P	R	I	Z	E	I	A
S	S	B	R	A	N	C	H	F	T	D
H	T	O	R	P	H	A	N	F	J	O
Y	E	H	O	R	R	I	B	L	E	P
X	R	F	A	R	M	M	I	S	S	T

4 Match these halves of sentences to describe Matthew's death in Chapter 6, and write them out in a paragraph.

1 When Anne arrived back at Green Gables,

2 Marilla was worried about him,

3 And the next morning, when Matthew opened a letter from the bank,

4 The letter said that all the Cuthberts' money was gone,

5 Anne and Marilla tried to help him,

6 because he had heart trouble.

7 Matthew looked much older, and Anne knew at once that something was wrong.

8 but it was too late, and Matthew was already dead.

9 and the bad news was too much for Matthew's heart.

10 his face went grey, and he fell to the ground.

5 **What do you think happened after the end of this story? Perhaps Marilla and her old friend Rachel Lynde had a conversation like this, about five years later. Complete their conversation. (Use one word for each space.)**

both, come, exciting, girl, happy, leave, live, looked, marry, miss, sad, stay, sure

MRS LYNDE: Well, Marilla, this is _____ news, isn't it?

MARILLA: Yes, but it's _____ for me, because it means that Anne will _____ Green Gables. I'll _____ her a lot!

MRS LYNDE: Of course, but she and Gilbert will _____ and see you very often, I'm _____!

MARILLA: Oh yes, Anne's a good _____. She's _____ after me well all this time. Poor Matthew! He'd be very _____ to see his little Anne _____ young Gilbert Blythe in Avonlea church!

MRS LYNDE: Where are Anne and Gilbert going to _____?

MARILLA: They're going to find a house near here, because Anne wants to _____ in Avonlea, and look after me.

MRS LYNDE: Well, I hope they'll _____ be very happy!

ABOUT THE AUTHOR

Lucy Maud Montgomery (1874–1942) was born in Canada, on Prince Edward Island. Her mother died when she was two years old, and she went to live with her grandmother and grandfather on their farm. She became a teacher for a short time, but after her grandfather died, she stopped teaching and helped her grandmother on the farm. By the 1890s, Lucy was already earning some money from her writing. In 1911, she married a churchman, the Reverend Ewan MacDonald, and went to live in Ontario.

She wrote her first book, *Anne of Green Gables*, in 1908, and it was an immediate success. Anne's life is very like the life of Lucy Montgomery, and Green Gables is very like her grandparents' house. If you go to Prince Edward Island, you can visit the old farmhouse where they lived. Between 1909 and 1939, Lucy Montgomery wrote six more books about Anne, starting with *Anne of Avonlea*. In these books, Anne grows up and has a family of her own. Lucy Montgomery also wrote books about another girl called Emily.

Her books have always been very popular, and people have made films and television programmes about *Anne of Green Gables*. The story is a hundred years old, but girls still enjoy it today, because they still think and feel like Anne, who is a very strong character.

OXFORD BOOKWORMS LIBRARY

Classics • Crime & Mystery • Factfiles • Fantasy & Horror
Human Interest • Playscripts • Thriller & Adventure
True Stories • World Stories

The OXFORD BOOKWORMS LIBRARY provides enjoyable reading in English, with a wide range of classic and modern fiction, non-fiction, and plays. It includes original and adapted texts in seven carefully graded language stages, which take learners from beginner to advanced level. An overview is given on the next pages.

All Stage 1 titles are available as audio recordings, as well as over eighty other titles from Starter to Stage 6. All Starters and many titles at Stages 1 to 4 are specially recommended for younger learners. Every Bookworm is illustrated, and Starters and Factfiles have full-colour illustrations.

The OXFORD BOOKWORMS LIBRARY also offers extensive support. Each book contains an introduction to the story, notes about the author, a glossary, and activities. Additional resources include tests and worksheets, and answers for these and for the activities in the books. There is advice on running a class library, using audio recordings, and the many ways of using Oxford Bookworms in reading programmes. Resource materials are available on the website <www.oup.com/bookworms>.

The *Oxford Bookworms Collection* is a series for advanced learners. It consists of volumes of short stories by well-known authors, both classic and modern. Texts are not abridged or adapted in any way, but carefully selected to be accessible to the advanced student.

You can find details and a full list of titles in the *Oxford Bookworms Library Catalogue* and *Oxford English Language Teaching Catalogues*, and on the website <www.oup.com/bookworms>.

THE OXFORD BOOKWORMS LIBRARY
GRADING AND SAMPLE EXTRACTS

STARTER • 250 HEADWORDS

present simple – present continuous – imperative –
can/cannot, must – going to (future) – simple gerunds ...

Her phone is ringing – but where is it?

Sally gets out of bed and looks in her bag. No phone. She looks under the bed. No phone. Then she looks behind the door. There is her phone. Sally picks up her phone and answers it. *Sally's Phone*

STAGE 1 • 400 HEADWORDS

... past simple – coordination with *and, but, or* –
subordination with *before, after, when, because, so* ...

I knew him in Persia. He was a famous builder and I worked with him there. For a time I was his friend, but not for long. When he came to Paris, I came after him – I wanted to watch him. He was a very clever, very dangerous man. *The Phantom of the Opera*

STAGE 2 • 700 HEADWORDS

... present perfect – *will* (future) – *(don't) have to, must not, could* –
comparison of adjectives – simple *if* clauses – past continuous –
tag questions – *ask/tell* + infinitive ...

While I was writing these words in my diary, I decided what to do. I must try to escape. I shall try to get down the wall outside. The window is high above the ground, but I have to try. I shall take some of the gold with me – if I escape, perhaps it will be helpful later. *Dracula*

STAGE 3 • 1000 HEADWORDS

… should, may – present perfect continuous – *used to* – past perfect –
causative – relative clauses – indirect statements …

Of course, it was most important that no one should see
Colin, Mary, or Dickon entering the secret garden. So Colin
gave orders to the gardeners that they must all keep away
from that part of the garden in future. *The Secret Garden*

STAGE 4 • 1400 HEADWORDS

… past perfect continuous – passive (simple forms) –
would conditional clauses – indirect questions –
relatives with *where/when* – gerunds after prepositions/phrases …

I was glad. Now Hyde could not show his face to the world
again. If he did, every honest man in London would be
proud to report him to the police. *Dr Jekyll and Mr Hyde*

STAGE 5 • 1800 HEADWORDS

… future continuous – future perfect –
passive (modals, continuous forms) –
would have conditional clauses – modals + perfect infinitive …

If he had spoken Estella's name, I would have hit him. I was
so angry with him, and so depressed about my future, that I
could not eat the breakfast. Instead I went straight to the old
house. *Great Expectations*

STAGE 6 • 2500 HEADWORDS

… passive (infinitives, gerunds) – advanced modal meanings –
clauses of concession, condition

When I stepped up to the piano, I was confident. It was as if I
knew that the prodigy side of me really did exist. And when
I started to play, I was so caught up in how lovely I looked
that I didn't worry how I would sound. *The Joy Luck Club*

The Children of the New Forest

CAPTAIN MARRYAT

Retold by Rowena Akinyemi

England in 1647: King Charles is in prison, and Cromwell's men are fighting the King's men. These are dangerous times for everybody.

The four Beverley children have no parents; their mother is dead and their father died while fighting for the King. Now Cromwell's soldiers have come to burn the house – with the children in it.

The four of them escape into the New Forest – but how will they live? What will they eat? And will Cromwell's soldiers find them?

Huckleberry Finn

MARK TWAIN

Retold by Diane Mowat

Who wants to live in a house, wear clean clothes, be good, and go to school every day? Not young Huckleberry Finn, that's for sure. So Huck runs away, and is soon floating down the great Mississippi River on a raft. With him is Jim, a black slave who is also running away. But life is not always easy for the two friends.

And there's 300 dollars waiting for anyone who catches poor Jim . . .